# WORDINGS OF HEART

## THOUSAND THOUGHTS IN MIND, SILENCE IN WORDS.

SUMAN MEENA

ISBN 979-888591121-4

# Contents

# Contents

*"I have never started a poem yet whose end I knew. Writing a poem is discovery."*

*- Robert Frost*

# Preface

Poetry is nothing, but the wordings of heart, always hard to find. These are poems written from deep within my heart. That's how the title came for this book "Wordings of Heart". The Book has words conveying emotions in poetic way, which you might relate too. Many of us have faced a situation where we want to express ourself when heartbroken but we are just not able to. At times we are afraid to express and sometimes we don't have proper words to speak about it. Our heart starts feel that heaviness and load. Just let the words flow from your heart. This Book contains that emotions that are left unspoken inside the heart. Letting emotions suppress within really feels painful. Here in this book, I releases all my thoughts that are trapped within and put those words to paper to share with you. I wrote this book during the times in life when felt most alone. And every poem is the outcome of emotion felt at that very moment. I hope! you as reader enjoy reading it as much as I enjoy writing it.

> "*Read every phrase with your heart, as every word written here is punctuated with emotions.*"

# Acknowledgements

Writing a book is harder than I thought and more rewarding than I could have ever imagined. Having an idea and turning it into a book is as hard as it sounds. the experience is both internally challenging and rewarding. None of this could have been possible without YourQuote team who let the writers bloom. Publishing is a writers ultimate dream and here writing my own published book with my name printed is really very exciting and I heartily thank the publication for this. Also, I'm eternally grateful to my friends - Priyanshi, Kayra, Liana and Janet who first appreciate my writings and encouraged me to write more and are always there with me. Thank You for being my life's precious part my dear friend. And most important of all. Thank You Almigthy! for your blessings of this art which make my emotions into strength and me a much better person than yesterday.

Thank You!

# Acknowledgements

*Suman Meena*

# About The Author

Suman is a character destined on a way to make people smile. A simple soul who has never betrayed anyone and a friendly girl who loves to read, write and paint. She finds true peace by expressing herself through poetry. Everyone calls her Angel. "Musings of Silent Eyes" is her recently first published book. She believes that while life is tough, there is always a happy ending just around the corner. Her principle is that following the voice of your heart will lead to that words that long to escape. She is now lost in the journey of finding herself and the purpose of her birth. Read her writings on Instagram: wordings.of.heart

# Who Am I

I'm not who you think to be
But, I'm the girl who is
Quiet in large groups
I'm the girl who greet the people
With a genuine smile
And the hardest person to offend
I'm the girl who loves to think
Rather than talking too much
I'm the girl who wanna peaceful life
with no hatred and love all around
I'm the girl who understands
Other person's words and feelings
Before taking any judgement
I'm the girl who is
Puffed with emotionality
And a girl with kind heart
I'm the girl who like floating wind
And want to float around
I'm the girl who cares
Loved ones the most
And hate society irrationality
I'm the girl who loves
The song sung by rain
And wanna be the smile

Of someone's face
I'm the girl who may be
The face you see in the streets
But not the soul i.e underneath
I'm the girl who adore
The simplicity in and out the most
And life for her is to
Search the purpose here
And to help human kind
Though She is strong
But sometimes cries like child
& One can easily find a
True friend in her with whom
Can share the deepest fears of life
Don't judge her
When you see me weak
Because you still don't know
What all she have got.

# 1. Far Away

Far away from here
Beyond the staring eyes & hatred
Wanna go somewhere
In a calm & solitude place
Away from cage of anguish
Away from the realm of dejection
To a place where love blossoms
Where there is no stress in life

Far away from here
Wanna go somewhere
Where everything seems crystal clear
Where there is no negativity
Where there exists a world where
People's heart filled with compassion

Wanna go to a place
Near the twinkling star
Where sky is painted with
Dreamland & happiness all around
To a place where nobody knows me.

# 2. Eternal Memories

As I stare up into the sky
Everything that surrounds me
Disappear into the enveloping darkness
I find myself wondering
I know you aren't anymore now
But your presence
Still lingers in my mind
When I look at the corners of house
The memories of you
Flood back infront of me
& Reminds me of you daily
In the crisp of air, I hear
Some notes of your voice
Calm and gentle breeze
Looks like a slight touch of yours
In my silence, I feel you
In my eyes, pictures of you roll back
And are always open
In dreamland to see you
I've nothing to lose
You left me a countless memories
& Never ending words to write
But the realization

That you are no longer here
Will always cause me pain
People said wrong
That you are not here
Because I know;
You're forever in my heart
Until we meet again.

# 3. Betrayals Hurts

I'm still wondering
Did you loved me
Even for a single moment
Did you cared me
Wholeheartedly
Maybe you did
When you got all that
you needed from me

But, dear friend
Your beautiful lies
Shake me slowly
As they break My heart
Into pieces
At last I thank You
To show me
What was the truth
And what was the real.

# 4. The Walls of My Room

The walls of my room
Often talk about the memories
that hanged there
And Heart captured once
It often talks about
My tears also
Confined within the
Walls of my room
And I learned to glow
In the gloom.

# 5. Letter to the World

This is my letter to the world
The letter without an address
The letter I have revised
For hundreds of times
The letter containing
Empty spaces and narrow lanes
The letter folded with precision
In the form of origami
But never opened.

# 6. Sit in Dark

I sit in the dark night alone
Below the huge blue sky
Talking to the moon
I trying get to reach you
In the countless star
Trying to find you

Listening to my favorite songs
Sitting in silence
Remembering the days
When I was living the
Most beautiful part of my life
When we used to talk
For the whole night
I still remember everything

You take away the best of me
Along with you Leaving us all behind
You departed from this life
Without even saying a word
I want to be in another place

Where no one could apart us
I want to go back to those simpler times
When everything was fine.

# 7. A Lost Soul

Detached herself
From everyone
Now,
She is wandering alone
With her loneliness.
To journey of
Finding a better self.

# 8. Nobody Knows

Nobody knows how hurted I'm
The real smile of mine
has been left far behind
Nobody knows my tears, my pain
Even if I'm laughing with all
The pain which is inside me
Hurting deep my soul.
Nobody knows how painful it is
When the heart is trapped
In the mystery of thoughts
Only I know
How much I need you
I kept my pain in the heaviest rain
But deep inside, I feel like crying
When I'm all alone.
Behind the fake smile living a life
Which is just hell without you.

# 9. A Broken Soul

A Broken Soul
Filled with emotions
Yet; carries strong desires
And is strong enough
To handle her pain
Fights with the world
With bare feet
Endures all the pain
With a beautiful smile
Bruised all her emotions
In a coffin
Along with her broken pieces
Now,
Searching for herself
Gathering all her
Strengths and will.

# 10. You and Me

I Feel your presence
Stronger in my heart
And deeper in my soul
When I whisper your name
In the silence of the night.

The light of you surrounds me
The love of you enfolds me
The power of you protects me
The presence of you watches over me.

# 11. There is One Thing

There is one thing I know for sure;
That one day, you'll search for me
All of your life
You gonna miss my vibes
But that day will be too late.

That day will be too late to regret
And to realize the worth of me
You'll be left with the things you never had
The courage to say before.

There is one thing I know for sure;
That one day, you'll lose the
Special vibes that gives meaning
To everything in your life
In the blink of an eye, everything
Gonna be change that day
And you'll never have that chance
To meet me again.

There is one thing I know for sure;
That one day, when you wake up,
You find me gone
There is one thing I know for sure;
That one day, once the story is over,
It gonna burn you; not now,
But someday for sure.

# 12. Love that Never Fades

Falling leaves turning the season
Sunset death to heavens eternal morn
Like a star, you're now far away
Both don't know the reason of separation
All the time, you're always
In my mind and heart
And there you'll always stays
You're my sunshine on a cloudy day
You're like the air I breathe
You're all I need in this world
You're like a special soul
Whom I meet in this lifetime

Each & every hello always has its goodbyes
But there is no letting go in ours
As, our love is pure and true
Will become perennial again some day
Then we've sweet escape to an island of sea
Where there is no separation
And we'll be forever each others.

# 13. Forever Connected

I'm connected with you
By the way of emotion
I'm connected with you
By the way of expression
I'm connected with you
By the way of caring
I'm connected with you
Beyond friendship
As I'm connected with you
on such a deep level
That no one can remove.

# 14. Easy to Say

It's easy to say sorry
But it's hard to forget things
It's easy to say be brave
And strong
But it's hard to remain resilient
It's easy to say didn't notice
Any notification from your side
But it's hard to feel
How it can hurt someone
It's easy to say I wanted
But I didn't stop
But it's hard to move on
Everything hurts
And everything burns
When you ignore
Someone's feelings.

# 15. I Wish

You are gone now
But my eyes
Always wishes to see you
And my ears
Always wishes to listen you
One more time
I can sense your presence
In my heart; Though you are
Far away from me
& I'll wait with silent passion
For one gesture, one glance from you
As I only find the spark of my life
In the silence of your love.

# 16. All I Need

All I need is you
To hold my hand
Through dark of life
& Encourage me
To go forth.

# 17. Time Flies

The time we spend together
Were the one I wanted most to stay
But the time never stops,
It keeps constantly moving
It slip beyond my grasp
When I want to hold onto it
As long as possible
It rolls so quickly that the
Beautiful moments we make
Get forever locked
In my heart as memories
The More it Goes,
The More it Takes Far Away
The Moment We Shared
Now, You Exists in My Writings
Where I Can Find You
You're No Longer Far From Me
Bcz You're Always in My Thoughts
You Exists Somewhere Inside Me
And You are with me until I die.

# 18. All Alone

Sitting in a crowd
Surrounded by people
But still I'm all alone
And Looking for a
Familiar face
With whom I can
Comfort myself.

# 19. Ending Day

Ending day leaves behind
Flashback memories
Ending day leaves behind
Droplets of dried tears
Ending day leaves behind
Footprints of loved ones
Ending day leaves behind
Lingering fragrances of the day
Ending day leaves behind
A hope for better tomorrow.

# 20. Feeling of Numbness

Feeling empty
Why? I don't know
Hugging a pillow
& Crying from inside
Why? I don't know
Scrolling the contacts
On whatsapp, at late night
Why? I don't know
Mind suddenly filled with
Thoughts and fears
Hugging the pillow again
With unstoppable tears
& Sleep listening to music.

# 21. Preferring Silence

There is lots to say
But; I'm preferring silence
There is lots I Know
But; I'm preferring silence
I'm preferring silence
Because, I'm tired now
Tired of explaining things
To people whom my words
Are worthless to understand
I'm writing thinking
Going through my mind
Being still, quiet
& Reserved within
I'm preferring silence
To live my life
And enjoying the doing
Not caring about
Anything else right now.

# 22. It's Not Easy

It's not easy to forget
What hurts the most
The betrayals I received
From those whom
I once thought to be mine
Also,
It's not easy to forget
What I loved the most
Those special moments
Which I kept close to heart
It's hard to forget the war
I've fought in the friendship
It's easier to create new one
But hard to forget past one.

# 23. Everything Changes

Everything gets change
With the passage of time
Nothing remains the same
After losing the interest
Even the Taste of people
Changes with the time
Relations can easily shattered
Once misunderstanding Comes
In between two lives
& Can't be resolved like before
As Nothing ever stays the same.

# 24. Lonely Walk

Walking alone in the street
Holding you in the thoughts
I trying to find a solitude place
But unable to find a single place
Where I can find some peace within
And it's difficult to let it go away
The wandering thoughts of mind
The pain of losing you is strong
And I'm unable to forget
You and those happy moments
In this world, without you
Me and my heart feeling lonely.

# 25. One Day

One day, we'll be at a place
Where there is no societal norms
Where no one can apart us
Black days will run away
And everything will be okay
That day, you'll be mine
My world will be like heaven
Our life will be a brighter day
I'll hold you for lifetime
& We'll be each other's forever.

# 26. Void

The colors have disappeared
The Music sounds like noise
The soul rhythm lost its way
The loneliness now shadow me.

Tears on my pillow and sadness on my face; is all what I'm left with. Till now, my heart is not ready to believe that you are not here, that you were an illusion. You walked in like a angel sent by god but now disappeared like that you were just a mirage. I still feel the void but new me is now stronger.

# 27. Haunted House

My mind is a haunted house
As it's foundations creak every night
Under the weight of
Darkest thoughts and deepest feelings

Every night it cries for whom
My existence won't matter
And fear creeps over me at that moment
By the thought of losing everything
That I have now

Past memories start to roll
All hours of the night in the mind
And try to entrap me in it
To imprison me in the past horrors
From inner, I feel like terrified
And everything looks then strange.

# 28. Chocolaty Me

I'm like a chocolate
Opened the innocence to the world
But the world is
Hundred steps ahead of my feelings
As I'm sweet to everyone
As I have a soft heart like chocolate
Which melts easily
That's why people hurt me more.

# 29. Need Somebody

In search of somebody
Who can understand me
And love me at my worst
Need somebody
Who can see my worth
And accept me as I'm
And never leave me alone
Whatever be the circumstances.

# 30. Silent Cry

Heart is crying
Bcz of the death of its fantasies
Everything is going well
But the heart still upset
And feeling like hopeless inside
Knows very well that
Fantasies get vanished someday
And crying is invalid for that
Yet,
My heart cries on such false things.

# 31. Alone in the Dark

You used to call me angel
& Comfort me with your words
You'll always be the one
I always cared & put high
Instead, I heard goodbye
A priority in your life
And a forever hand
That is all what I wanted
Instead, I heard goodbye
There's nothing I can do now
Perhaps, you have made
Your choice and moved on.

# 32. Broken Friendship

My friendship with you
Turned to dust & Ash
When I lost all love
And Care from you
Your story shows me
How little I meant to you
I feel Loneliness Upon the
Hours of Every midnight
And it hurts so badly
That my presence won't matter
To You now; And
You walk away from life
Even without a talk.

# 33. Hurts

Somedays, I walked alone
& Somedays, I took to the road
Everywhere I went
Carried an ache with me

I Understand that love and relationships
Are tied with delicate thread
But, if someone is always ignorant
Then, we must let them go away.

# 34. Ignorance

You didn't have time to text me
May be you are busy somewhere else
Which is more imporatnt than me
I'm such a big fool
Who kept tearing her soul to pieces

My feelings for you go away
As you don't understand my worth
And now,
I myself ended up everything
As the heart that always understands
Get tired now because
You don't value my emotions

And Now,
I'm dead for those breaths
Who have problems with my words
& For those who don't care my feelings.

# 35. I Thought

I wanna text you
But I don't know what I would say
It's been a long time
Since we just talked to each other
Just one word,
would make it right once again
But I don't know
If you're feeling the same way
Or if it's me only
Who is wishing that you'll stay.

I wanna call you
But I'm scared
Would you still take my call?
Or just leave it like the other day
Or would you call me back?
As it's been a long time
Since we were close.

# 36. End

I was badly hurt
But I didn't say anything to those
Where my emotions have
No value and my words are dumb
I forget myself
Getting lost in your love
But now, your presence
Won't affect me anymore
As I lost the feelings for you.

9 798885 911214

Printed by Libri Plureos GmbH in Hamburg, Germany